koopmanrareart.com

Timeless Masterpieces in the Digital Age

Koopman Rare Art 2014

53/64 Chancery Lane
London WC2A 1QS

+44 (0) 20 7242 7624
enquiries@koopmanrareart.com
www.koopmanrareart.com

Koopman Rare Art at Masterpiece, London, July 2013

FOREWORD

IN MANY WAYS COLLECTING ART AND ANTIQUES is rather like sport, and as anyone who follows sport knows there are two things that lead to success: you need to have just a little of Lady Luck on your side; and the more you practise the easier it becomes – or so it seems.

At Koopman Rare Art, we spend most of our time searching for great silver like the items you will find in this catalogue. We know that exciting objects such as these stand out as works of art on grounds of quality, art-historical significance and historical importance. For discerning collectors today provenance is paramount and so historical research is central to our business.

With that in mind, and all our efforts (round the clock!) to find the best wherever it surfaces on the globe, we still need a little luck to be in the right place at the right time. Perhaps the more we work the luckier we become.

This catalogue is rather unusual. The format we chose is a clear sign that electronic media have become an efficient, and indeed crucial, tool for us today, both to buy and to sell. We have spent a great deal of time too in shaping and improving our website, as well as in keeping it up to date. In short, we have come to realise that even though our life is devoted to old things, modern technology can still help!

Some of the most exceptional and interesting objects we have purchased in the last twelve months are featured in our catalogue. Some items, alas, we have already sold. Our ownership of beautiful objects, whilst often brief, gives us much pleasure.

This catalogue then is both forward-looking and retrospective in more ways than one.

The magnificent ambassadorial wine-coolers on p. 24 celebrate their three hundredth birthday this year. How many things produced today will still be functional – and beautiful – in 2314? We hope that you will feel that history is alive as you look at these wonderful treasures from the past.

Lewis Smith
lewis@koopmanrareart.com

An evocation of the East

1. An Important Charles II Chinoiserie Porringer on Stand

Silver
London, 1684
Maker's mark of **John Ruslen**
Height (porringer): 8 ½ in (21.5 cm)
Diameter (tazza): 14 in (35.2 cm)
Weight: 75 oz 15 dwt (2,360 g)
Scratch weights: *43=12* on porringer; *33=15* on stand

HERALDRY
The arms are those of Buckland, Somerset.

Chinoiserie, that romantic evocation of the East, appears in English decorative arts from time to time. Flat-chased decoration like this, of extravagant warriors and sages, exotic birds and luscious foliage, occurs briefly on silver made in the 1680s, and shows us how craftsmen of the time imagined Asia. Some years ago, Carl Dauterman, the curator of the Metropolitan Museum of Art, suggested that one specialized workshop carried out this decoration, although the pieces are struck with various makers' marks. More recently, however, scholars such as Philippa Glanville and David Mitchell have noted differences in style and handling and it now seems certain that there was more than one studio carrying out chinoiserie decoration.

This porringer with its original stand is distinguished by the high quality of the chasing, comparable to that on several monteiths (or scalloped punch bowls) in the Milwaukee Art Museum, the Ashmolean, the Victoria and Albert Museum and elsewhere which can be attributed to the same hand. The lively horses on this example are a rare feature on chinoiserie silver.

The Buckland arms appear on a fine twelve-sided porringer and cover of 1655 in the Fogg Art Museum, Harvard University.

Chinoiserie by de Lamerie

2. A George II Chinoiserie Tea Caddy

Silver
London, 1746
Maker's mark of **Paul de Lamerie**
Height: 5 ½ in (14 cm)
Weight: 14 oz 10 dwt (455 g)

HERALDRY
The crest is that of Watson below the initial *W*.

The second great wave of chinoiserie appears in English silver in the 1740s and 50s. Unlike the quirky flat-chased designs of the 1680s, however, this decoration was embossed in high relief and presents a happy blending of European foliage and much more authentic Asian motifs. The decoration on this tea caddy, which first appears on a handful of examples from Paul de Lamerie's workshop, has been studied by Peter Kaellgren, curator emeritus of the Royal Ontario Museum. In the following decade a number of other silversmiths including Thomas Heming, the Royal Goldsmith, copied the form.

Parisian perfection

3. A Magnificent Soup Tureen on Stand from the Orloff Service

Silver
Paris, 1770
Maker's mark of **Jacques-Nicolas Roettiers**
Length (bowl): 17 ¼ in (43.5 cm)
Length of base: 19 ¾ in (50 cm)
Weight: 384 oz 10 dwt (11,960 g)

PROVENANCE
Catherine II, Empress of Russia (1729–1796)
Given to Count Gregory Orloff (1734–1783) in 1772
Catherine II, reacquired in 1784, and by descent in the imperial collections to Czar Nicolas II (1868–1918) until 1917
Soviet Government until 1929
Private Monegasque collection until 2013

The Orloff Service is one of the most famous of the royal services produced for the courts of Europe by the great Paris goldsmiths of the eighteenth century. Its monumental classicism is tempered by a Parisian elegance. The neo-classical sculptor Etienne-Maurice Falconet acted as the middleman in the commissioning of the service from the Roettiers workshop in Paris, and he may have been involved with its design. Falconet first came to the Russian court in 1766 having been commissioned to create the gigantic equestrian bronze

sculpture of Peter the Great which is one of the principal sights of St Petersburg.

Eventually some 3,000 pieces were made including eight pots à oille, eight tureens, forty-eight pairs of candlesticks, forty-eight dozen plates, thousands of pieces of cutlery and numerous dishes. The empress ordered more in 1771, including warmers, chocolate pots and milk jugs. In his *Inventories of the Silver of the Court of His Imperial Highness*, published in 1907, Baron Foelkersam estimated the total cost of the service to have amounted to £1,200,000.

The Roettiers, father and son, were goldsmiths to the king, Louis XV. Originally from Antwerp, Jacques, the father, had trained in the workshop of Thomas Germain. Jacques's son Jacques-Nicolas first joined the workshop as an apprentice in 1752, and then as a partner after becoming master in 1765. After the closure of the Germain workshop, the Roettiers were the last goldsmiths living in the Louvre. Both worked actively for the king and his entourage, making a table service for Louis XV and a gold dinner service for Madame du Barry.

Gregory Orloff, favourite of Catherine, had led the coup which secured her on the throne as sole ruler and empress of Russia. He had become her lover but while she was extremely fond of him, she was unwilling to marry him or to give him a political role. However, she lavished him with titles, lands and gifts.

By the time the service was delivered to her in Russia, the empress had become disenchanted with Count Orloff, who had been instructed to negotiate peace with the Turks at Fokchany. She dismissed him from his diplomatic mission and, as a parting gift, she gave him the Roettiers silver service. The count was always to keep the service with him, even taking it into exile in Holland. Upon hearing of his death in 1783 Catherine,

Count Gregory Orloff (1734–1783), engraving.
Private Collection

saddened by the news, wrote to Baron Frederick Grimm that although she had prepared herself for this eventuality, her pain was immense. She bought the service back.

Afterwards the service was kept in the imperial collection. By 1907 only 842 pieces were accounted for in Foelkersam's inventories. In 1917 after the Revolution, the service became the property of the Russian government who started selling it piece by piece from 1920 onwards. Today only some two hundred pieces of this vast service are known, and this tureen is the largest and one of the last to have remained in private hands.

Restoration opulence

4. An Important Charles II Sideboard Dish

Silver
London, 1674
Maker's mark of **Thomas Jenkins**
Diameter: 19 ¼ in (49 cm)
Weight: 70 oz 15 dwt (2,200 g)

HERALDRY
The crest is that of Corbet, as borne by Captain Richard Corbet (1649–1718). The Corbet family is one of a small group of families that can trace its descent back in an unbroken line to a Norman who came over with William the Conqueror.

PROVENANCE
Captain Richard Corbet of Shawbury Park and Moreton Corbet (1649–1718)
Andrew Corbet (d. 1757)
Andrew Corbet (1720–1796)
Richard Prynce Corbet (1735–1779)
Sir Andrew Corbet, 1st Bt. (1766–1835)
Sir Andrew Vincent Corbet, 2nd Bt. (1800–1855)
Sir Vincent Rowland Corbet, 3rd Bt. (1821–1891)
Sir Walter Corbet, 4th Bt. (1856–1897), inherited by his widow
Caroline Douglas, daughter of Captain James Stewart, 11th Hussars, who married as her second husband Reginald Astley (1862–1942), Alresford, Hampshire
Private English Collection

This dish was part of a suite of silver commissioned by Captain Richard Corbet. The group includes a fine porringer and cover of 1672 engraved with the same crest within a similar cartouche, now in the Irwin Untermyer Collection in the Metropolitan Museum of Art, New York.

The maker's mark TI with two escallops (shells) between the initials was long thought to be that of Thomas Issod. The mark appears on some of the most impressive pieces of post-Restoration plate. Thomas Issod, however, was found some years ago to have been a specialist spoon-maker, and thanks to extensive detective work in the archives of the Goldsmiths' Company in London, Arthur Grimwade and Judith Bannister in the 1970s discovered that the identity of this important maker was in fact Thomas Jenkins.

One of the most important Restoration silversmiths, Jenkins had a broad output including many large pieces of display plate of which this sideboard dish is a good example. The high-quality and bold chasing of Jenkins's work is much in evidence in the scenes set in cartouches of the Four Elements, probably based on Netherlandish prints. The scenes of putti should be compared with the scenes chased on a pair of unmarked altar dishes in the Tower of London, dating from the early 1660s and attributed to Jean Cooqus, the Flemish immigrant silver worker. It is known that Cooqus had some of his work submitted for assay by others.

A highly important Italian Renaissance tazza

5. The Aldobrandini Vespasian Tazza

Silver gilt
Milan, c. 1560–80
Height 15 ¼ in (38.5 cm)
Weight: 90 oz (2,799 g)

PROVENANCE
Cardinal Pietro Aldobrandini (1571–1621), recorded in his 1603 inventory, *to his sister*
Olimpia Aldobrandini (1567–1637), *to her son*
Cardinal Ippolito Aldobrandini (1592–1638), recorded in his posthumous inventory in 1638, *to his niece*
Olimpia Aldobrandini-Borghese (1623–1682), Princess of Rossano, *to her son*
Giovanni Battista Pamphili (1648–1709), Duke of Carpineto, recorded in his posthumous inventory in 1710
In 1769 to the Borghese branch of the family
In 1826 with the retail silversmith Kensington Lewis, St James's St, London
With the retail goldsmith Thomas Hamlet, Princes St, London, *his sale*
George Robins (auctioneer), London, February 3, 1834, as by Benvenuto Cellini (1,000 guineas to Emanuel, probably Emanuel Brothers, Bevis Marks, St Mary Axe, London)
Charles Scarisbrick, Scarisbrick Hall, Lancashire, *his posthumous sale*
Christie's, London (auctioneers), May 15, 1861, lot 159, as attributed to Benvenuto Cellini; sold to Richard Attenborough, silversmith of the Strand
Frédéric Spitzer, Paris, *his sale*
Paul Chevallier and Charles Mannheim (auctioneers), Paris, April 17–June 16, 1893, lot 1761
By 1901 J. Pierpont Morgan (1837–1913), *to his son*
J.P. Morgan (1867–1943), and by descent
The Morgan Collection, Christie's, New York, October 26, 1982, lot 68
Private Collection, Kentucky, until 2012

EXHIBITED
London, 1902, Burlington Fine Arts Club, Burlington House, London, 1901, case F. no. 2

PUBLISHED
A. Darcel, *La Collection Spitzer. Antiquité, moyen-âge, renaissance*, Paris, 1890–2, vol. III: *Orfèvrerie civile*, pp. 23–4
Illustrated Catalogue of Silversmith's Work, European, Burlington Fine Arts Club, 1901, p. 55, pl. LXXIV
E. Alfred Jones, *Illustrated Catalogue of the Collection of Old Plate of J. Pierpont Morgan*, London, 1908, p. 84, pl. LXXV

This tazza was originally part of a set of twelve, each one depicting one of the Twelve Caesars, which was described by the scholar John Hayward as "the most impressive single monument of Italian and perhaps of European goldsmiths' work of the sixteenth century." The rest of the set is divided among collections around the world including the Victoria and Albert Museum, London, the Metropolitan Museum of Art, New York,

as well as institutions in Lisbon, Madrid, Toronto and Minneapolis.

The Twelve Caesars, the most famous of the Roman emperors, were the subject of a book entitled *De Vita Caesarum* written in AD 121 by Gaius Suetonius Tranquillus, secretary to the Emperor Hadrian. A printed edition of the work was published for the first time in 1470 and went through numerous versions and translations including one by Erasmus of Rotterdam. The emperors were depicted on medals, engravings, Limoges painted enamels and silver.

Each tazza bowl is divided into four segments, each devoted to a narrative scene from the emperor's life, based on the relevant passage in Suetonius. In the centre a free-standing sculpture of the emperor surveys these scenes, which are chased in high relief.

The set was made for Cardinal Pietro Aldobrandini, one of the great collectors and patrons of late Renaissance Italy. Pietro's architectural patronage included the Villa Aldobrandini at Frascati, with its fabulous gardens and fountains, and he was a patron of Torquato Tasso, Frescobaldi, Domenichino and Guido Reni. His art collection, part of which still forms the basis of the Galleria Doria-Pamphilj in Rome, included works by Raphael and Mantegna. Research by Stefanie Walker a few years ago revealed that the set was recorded in a 1603 inventory of the cardinal's collection.

The set is recorded in London by 1826, when it was exhibited by Kensington Lewis, a retail goldsmith who specialized in antique plate and plate made in the antique taste. In 1834 the tazze were sold by the auctioneer G.H. Robins. They were next acquired by the collector and patron Charles Scarisbrick, an eccentric recluse who collected pictures, furniture, carvings and works of art, and employed the young A.W.N. Pugin to transform his house, Scarisbrick Hall, Lancashire, into a medieval fantasy. At Scarisbrick's death in 1860, most of his collections were sold to provide for his three illegitimate children.

The full set of the twelve emperors appeared at Christie's, London, on May 15, 1861 – the last time they were recorded together. After the sale, the set was broken up, with six of them, including this example, having their original feet replaced with more elaborate ones. These six were included in the auction held after the death of the Parisian dealer Frédéric Spitzer, whose mansion in the sixteenth *arrondissement* was known as the Musée Spitzer. After the 1893 auction, much of the Spitzer collection ended up going to American buyers. The Vespasian tazza was no exception, going to one of the most aggressive collectors of the day, J.P. Morgan.

The Aldobrandini Vespasian tazza has been requested for an exhibition bringing together the twelve emperors for the first time since the 1860s, planned by the Metropolitan Museum of Art.

A unique Storr design

6. A Pair of Unusual Regency Wine-Coolers

Silver
London, 1816
Maker's mark of **Paul Storr**, retailed by **Rundell, Bridge & Rundell**, the Royal Goldsmiths
Height: 8 ⅛ in (22.2 cm)
Weight: 221 oz (6,879 g)

HERALDRY
The arms are those of George Hay Dawkins-Penryhn of Penryhn Castle, Wales (d. 1840).

George Hay Dawkins-Penryhn, by Charles J. Basébé.
Courtesy of Christie's

These wine-coolers were originally part of an extensive service commissioned by one of the wealthiest men in Wales. The design is highly unusual, and was clearly a special commission from Rundell's.

George Dawkins Pennant inherited from his father's cousin Lord Penrhyn both extensive estates in North Wales, containing lucrative slate quarries, and plantations in Jamaica. He served as an MP for much of his adult life. Penryhn Castle, a neo-Norman-style castle with over 300 rooms, was created for him by the architect Thomas Hopper between 1821 and 1835. On his visit in 1841, Greville described it as "a vast pile of building, and certainly very grand, but altogether, though there are fine things and some good rooms in the house, the most gloomy place I ever saw, and I would not live there if they would make me a present of the castle".

Dawkins Pennant died at his London house in December 1840. He was succeeded in the Welsh and Jamaican estates, worth £80,000 a year, by his elder daughter Juliana and her husband Edward Gordon Douglas, who took the additional name of Pennant in 1841 and was created Lord Penrhyn in 1866. An enthusiastic obituarist wrote that Dawkins Pennant "possessed inviolable rectitude, scrupulous adherence to what he believed to be his duty, singleness of purpose, unobtrusive manners, and a benevolent heart".

Koopman Rare Art | 19

Suitable for an aristocrat

7. A George II Royal Christening Bowl and Cover

Silver
London, c. 1731
Maker's mark of **Edward Feline**
Width (over handles): 15 in (38.2 cm)
Weight: 159 oz 2 dwt (4,950 g)

The inscription reads *Lady Emilia Lenos Oct. 25th 1731*

HERALDRY
The royal arms are those of King George II.

PROVENANCE
King George II's christening gift to his goddaughter Lady Emilia (Emily) Lennox (1731–1814), daughter of Charles, second Duke of Richmond and Lennox (1701–1750), who became the wife of James, twentieth Earl of Kildare, created first Duke of Leinster and then by descent to Gerald, eighth Duke of Leinster (1914–2004) *His Grace the Duke of Leinster*, sale, Sotheby's, London, May 3, 1984, lot 75
His Excellency Mahdi Mohammed Altajir

EXHIBITED
London, 1989, *The Glory of the Goldsmith: Magnificent Gold and Silver from the Al-Tajir Collection*, no. 66

PUBLISHED
C. Truman, ed., *The Glory of the Goldsmith: Magnificent Gold and Silver from the Al-Tajir Collection*, 1989, p. 96

The elaborate nature of Emily Lennox's cup, with its heraldic ornament, sets it apart from other royal christening gifts of the period. While it was customary for the king to give his god-children a piece of plate for their christening, this usually took the form of a plainer cup and cover, two-handled and with a spool-shaped cover, which was sometimes accompanied by a stand. In this case however it seems that Emily's father had a hand in choosing the cup's design which advertises the royal nature of the gift with its use of the lion and unicorn as handles and the royal badge of a lion forming the finial. The only other instance of this highly unusual form is a cup presented by the king to Henry Vane on his marriage to Lady Grace Fitzroy in 1725, now in the Victoria and Albert Museum.

Lady Emily had been christened just over one month previously at St Margaret's Church, Westminster, her other god-parents being Princess Amelia, the king's second daughter, and Camilla, Countess of Tankerville. Emily was a distant cousin of the king, as her father was the grandson of King Charles II by his mistress Louise de Kérouaille, Duchess of Portsmouth.

Lady Emily's marriage to the ambitious Irish aristocrat James, twentieth Earl of Kildare, was at first opposed by her parents, their preference being an Englishman. However they overcame their reservations and the wedding was the talk of society. Emily and her three sisters were the subject of Stella Tillyard's best-selling book *Aristocrats: Caroline, Emily, Louisa and Sarah Lennox, 1740-1832*, published in 1994, and the subsequent film.

A royal "perk" of office

8. A Magnificent Sideboard Dish Celebrating the Coronation of Queen Anne

Silver gilt
London, 1702
Maker's mark of **John Bache**
Diameter: 25 in (63.5 cm)
Weight: 155 oz (4,832 g)

HERALDRY
The arms are those of Bertie with those of Wynn in pretence for Robert, fourth Earl of Lindsey (1660–1723) and his wife Mary, daughter and co-heir of Sir John Wynn, second baronet of Gwydir. He was created Marquess of Lindsey in 1706 and Duke of Ancaster and Kesteven in 1715.

PROVENANCE
Presented to Robert, fourth Earl of Lindsey in 1702
by descent to Montagu, twelfth Earl of Lindsey (1861–1938), Uffington House, Stamford
A Gentleman, Christie's, London, March 22, 1906, lot 121
John Pierpont Morgan (1837–1913)
The Morgan Sale, Parke-Bernet, New York, October 30–November 1, 1947, lot 165
An Arizona Collector
Christie's, New York, October 28, 1985, lot 234
His Excellency Mahdi Mohammed Altajir

EXHIBITED
London, 1989, *The Glory of the Goldsmith: Magnificent Gold and Silver from the Al-Tajir Collection*, no. 47

PUBLISHED
A Phillips, "A Royal Puzzle", *Christie's Review of the Season*, 1986, pp. 310–1
C. Truman, ed., *The Glory of the Goldsmith: Magnificent Gold and Silver from the Al-Tajir Collection*, 1989, p. 70, no. 47
C. Hartop, *The Huguenot Legacy: English Silver 1680–1760*, 1996, p. 82

The fourth Earl of Lindsey succeeded his father as Hereditary Lord Great Chamberlain on May 8, 1701. Bishop Burnet described his as 'a fine gentleman, hath both wit and learning'. Dean Swift felt otherwise, for in his copy of Burnet's *Works*, he wrote in the margin, 'I never observed a grain of either'.

In 1702, the Earl of Lindsey presided over the coronation of Queen Anne. As a perquisite of fulfilling this hereditary duty he received an ewer and two large basins which were cited in the Jewel Office records under "Coronation Claims":

> April 21, 1702, Delivered unto the Right Hon[ble]. The Earle of Lindsey, Lorde Greate Chamberlaine as Chief Officer of the Ewry as his Claime two large chased basons gilt, one chaced Ewre gilt – 355 oz. 4 dwt.

Lindsey's ewer, by Lewis Mettayer, remains at Grimsthorpe Castle. Another dish, presented to the Earl of Exeter after the coronation, is akin in size, weight and decoration to this dish.

Royal presentation wine-coolers

9. A Pair of Important George I Wine-Coolers

Silver
London, 1714
Maker's mark of **Lewis Mettayer**
Height: 9 ¼ in (23 cm)
Length over handles: 11 ½ in (29 cm)
Weight: 230 oz (7,160 g)
Scratch weights: *116 6* and *115 17*

HERALDRY

The arms are those of Sir Paul Methuen (1672–1757), the son of John Methuen (1650–1706), English envoy to Portugal and negotiator of the Methuen Treaty.

PROVENANCE

Issued to Paul Methuen by the Jewel Office in 1714, by descent to Field Marshall the Rt. Hon. Lord Methuen, Christie's, London, February 25, 1920, lot 45 (£826 11s 2d to Crichton Bros.)
Private French collection until 2010

EXHIBITED

London, 1928: *The Daily Telegraph Exhibition of Antiques and Works of Art*, Olympia, p. 250, lent by S.J. Phillips
London, 1928: *Exhibition of Art Treasures under the auspices of the British Antique Dealers' Association,* Grafton Galleries, p. 113, no. 968, lent by S.J. Phillips

PUBLISHED
The Daily Telegraph Exhibition of Antiques and Works of Art, Olympia, 1928, p. 250
Exhibition of Art Treasures under the auspices of the British Antique Dealers' Association, Grafton Galleries, p. 113, no. 968
M. Clayton, *The Collector's Dictionary of the Silver and Gold of Great Britain and North America*, rev. edn, London, 1985, plate 723

The year 2014 sees the three hundredth anniversary of the arrival of the Hanoverian dynasty. The new king George I, chosen by a junta of Whig grandees, was the obvious choice because of his religion and his descent from James I. He took his time in moving his retinue from Hanover to England but once arrived, new diplomatic initiatives were begun, and a flurry of ambassadors appointed. All this required new silver in the latest taste.

Sir Paul Methuen had continued the diplomatic work in Portugal begun by his father. England and Portugal had enjoyed close ties since the Middle Ages, and to this day the two countries have remained allies and have never been at war. Methuen senior had secured a treaty with Portugal in 1703 which reaffirmed the old fourteenth-century alliance, but it was the trade agreement signed at the same time which was to have long-lasting influence on the economy of both nations. The military campaigns of Louis XIV at the end of the seventeenth century had made it vital for England to keep a market for her wool and, denied access to French wines, to be able to buy Portugal's wines from Alentejo and the Douro Valley. To this we owe the development of port as "the Englishman's wine".

Paul Methuen had first travelled to Lisbon in 1691, when his father was appointed minister there. He gained valuable experience and the esteem of King Dom Pedro.

During two absences of his father he became chargé d'affaires, rising to Minister on his father's appointment as Lord Chancellor of Ireland. He succeeded his father as ambassador to Portugal on the latter's death in July 1706. In 1714 on the accession of George I, Methuen was appointed ambassador to Spain and Morocco, and for this mission he was granted the customary allowance of silver from the Jewel Office in order to entertain in the appropriate state while *en poste*. The royal warrant dated November 5, 1714 to Lord Guernsey, Master of His Majesty's Jewel Office, specified the allowance of 5,890 ounces of white plate and 1,066 ounces of silver gilt. The white plate was used for the first two courses, while the gilt plate appeared on the table for the "desart". The service was ready for delivery the following month, and the Delivery Book, now in the National Archives, lists the silver which includes, in addition to these "ice pailes" and the usual dishes and plates, "two chamber pots", "two small sconces", "two small sugar boxes",

Sir Paul Methuen K.B. (1672–1757), posthumous portrait by Adrien Carpentiers, oil on panel. *Corsham Court, Wiltshire/ The Bridgeman Art Library*

"a chocolate pott" and a "Bohea tea pot".

Silver issued by the Jewel Office was technically speaking loaned to the recipient to use while performing their office. But the office holder was often reluctant to return the silver and, in the case of ambassadors, there was usually a haggle over the payment of their expenses. A compromise was often reached which involved the ambassador being allowed to keep the silver in lieu of any cash payments. In Methuen's case, a few years after his return the king was "graciously pleased in Consideration of the many good and acceptable Services perform'd unto us by the said Paul Methuen to grant unto him the aforesaid Plate".

These wine-coolers are among the earliest of the form in Britain. Lewis Mettayer's master, fellow Huguenot David Willaume, made the earliest known pair for the Duke of Devonshire in 1698. The single bottle wine-cooler was an introduction from France after technological developments enabled glass blowers to produce cylindrical wine bottles that could be stored on their side, thus preventing the cork from drying out. Vintage wine was born.

Geometry for dining

10. An Unusual Decagonal Dish from the Speaker Smith Service

Silver
London, 1729
Maker's mark of **David Willaume II**
Diameter: 19 in (48.5 cm)
Weight: 105 oz 9 dwt (3,280 g)
Scratch weight: *114-3*

HERALDRY
The royal arms are those of Queen Anne; the crest is that of Smith.

PROVENANCE
Thomas Assheton-Smith and thence by descent to his great-nephew George William Duff of Vaenol, Caernarvonshire, who assumed the name Duff-Assheton-Smith in 1858 and then by descent to Sir Michael Duff, Bt., sale, Christie's, London, December 10, 1958, lot 129

In 1774 Thomas Assheton-Smith succeeded to the estates of his maternal uncle William Smith, the son of Speaker John Smith, who had been elected as Speaker of the House of Commons on October 24, 1705. As was customary, John Smith had been issued with 4,000 ounces of plate for his use whilst he held the office of Speaker. Smith held the post until November 1708 and the following October the plate was discharged (i.e. released for him to keep) as a perquisite of the office. Smith and his descendants continued to add to the service, ordering pieces in the plain Queen Anne style even though it would have become unfashionable. Interestingly, they continued to have the pieces engraved with the arms and initials of Queen Anne.

"The most munificent of all benefactors"

11. A Set of Four Fine George II Figural Candlesticks

Silver
London, 1750
Maker's mark of **Thomas Heming**, the Royal Goldsmith
Height: 11 ¼ in (28.6 cm)
Weight: 84 oz 15 dwt (2,640 g)

HERALDRY
The arms are those of Wasey impaling those of Spencer, as borne by Dr William Wasey who married Margaret, daughter of Gilbert Spencer. The other arms are those of the Royal College of Physicians.

PROVENANCE
Private English Collection since 1956

Dr Baldwin Hamey was "the most munificent of all the benefactors" of the Royal College of Physicians. On his death he left money so that "every President shall be presented with a piece of silver plate of above three score ounces". Dr William Wasey, who was physician to King George II, was elected President of the College in 1750 and the Cash Book for that year records:

> September 19 P^d. Y^e President 25 Pounds being ye annual donation of the late Dr Baldwin Hamey for a peice [sic] of Plate
>
> £25.0.0

The Treasurer of the college later reported that "the President had bought two pairs of chaised [sic] Candlesticks therewith".

Besides Thomas Heming, both Paul de Lamerie and Phillips Garden made candlesticks of this caryatid form. The fluid modelling of the bases, with their continuous movement, makes them some of the purest examples of the English rococo.

Koopman Rare Art | 31

Sculptural magnificence

12. A Monumental Regency Sideboard Dish

Silver gilt
London, 1814
Maker's mark of **William Pitts**, retailed by **Rundell, Bridge & Rundell**, the Royal Goldsmiths
Diameter: 22 ¼ in (56.2 cm)
Weight: 195 oz 10 dwt (6,080 g)

PROVENANCE
Mrs C. Kisielewski Dunbar, Sotheby's, London, June 11, 1970, lot 237
Collection of C. Ruxton Love and Audrey B. Love, Christie's, New York, October 19, 2004, lot 253

EXHIBITED
London, 2005, *Royal Goldsmiths: The Art of Rundell & Bridge, 1797–1843*, Koopman Rare Art, no. 27

PUBLISHED
V. Brett, *The Sotheby's Directory of Silver*, London, 1984, p. 259
A. Phillips and J. Sloane, *Antiquity Revisited: English and French Silver-Gilt from the Audrey Love Collection*, London, 1997, p. 50, no. 8
C. Hartop, *Royal Goldsmiths: The Art of Rundell & Bridge, 1797–1843*, exh. cat., Koopman Rare Art, London, 2005, p. 151, no. 27

This important dish is among the earliest examples of the revival of chased Renaissance display silver promoted by the Royal Goldsmiths, Rundell, Bridge & Rundell, which was to be enthusiastically taken up by the Prince Regent. The scene of the Feast of the Gods is based on a series of three bronze reliefs which have been attributed to Guglielmo della Porta.

Other versions of this dish include a pair of 1810 and 1812 in the Royal Collection, and another on loan to the Brighton Pavilion.

The first decade of the nineteenth century was a time of tremendous creativity in English silver, led by Rundell's, who operated a network of silversmiths, designers and chasers. They promoted the "Imperial" style, produced mainly in the workshop of Paul Storr, which mingled architectural motifs from both Greece and Rome on classical vase shapes. It was to the Pitts family studio that Rundell's turned for re-creations of Renaissance sculpture to be incorporated into pieces which revived the seventeenth-century tradition of grandiose circular and oval display dishes.

Interestingly, Rundell's sold dishes of this design to their leading clients, such as William Pole-Tylney-Long-Wellesley and the Marquess of Ormonde, before the Prince Regent purchased his two, the first in June 1811 and the second in October 1812. "In the field of plate [the Prince Regent] seems to have been content to follow rather than lead the field. In a curious inversion of the traditional practice of court patronage, the driving force in the design and production of innovative gold and silver work was the supplier,

Rundell's, and their market … [The Prince Regent] often bought plate after the model had already been produced and sold to other clients" (C. Hartop, *op. cit.*, p. 96).

Rundell's 1812 invoice to the Prince Regent describes one of his dishes as:

> A richly chased sideboard dish, to match His Royal Highnesses [*sic*], and with devices of the Feast of the Gods, from a design by Michael Angelo, with chased mosaic border, 284 oz. 15 dwt., fashion 12s oz. = £291/17/4; engraving crest and coronet, 9s; gilding all over dead and red, £96 (E. Alfred Jones, *The Gold and Silver of Windsor Castle*, 1911, p. 114)

William Pitts senior was the son of Thomas Pitts, a large-scale manufacturer of epergnes and other table silver for retailers such as Rundell's. From 1791 to 1799 William Pitts was in partnership with Joseph Preedy. In 1806 his son William had joined him as an apprentice and he went on to become one of the leading silver chasers of his time. He worked not only for Rundell's, for whom he chased at least one of the versions of the Achilles Shield, but also for their rivals, Green, Ward & Green, where he worked on Stothard's Wellington Shield. In 1812 he was awarded the Iris medal for modelling from the Society of Arts.

A protest against "necessitous strangers"

13. A Fine William III Cup and Cover

Silver gilt
London, 1700
Maker's mark of **John Bodington**
Height: 8 ⅝ in (22 cm)
Weight: 39 oz 10 dwt (1,244 g)

HERALDRY
The arms are those of Heyton.

John Bodington ran one of the most successful workshops in London at the end of the seventeenth century, producing silver matching the best productions of the Huguenot immigrants. The quality of the strapwork, or applied flat decoration, on this cup is superb, and the addition of cast beading on top of the strapwork is a feature that few workers could execute well. It is a myth that strapwork and other advanced techniques were innovations of the Huguenots, for they appear on English silver as early as the beginning of the 1660s. Little wonder then that Bodington and his fellow Londoners petitioned the Goldsmiths' Company in 1703 and again in 1711 complaining of unfair competition from foreign craftsmen, or 'necessitous strangers', who were willing to work longer hours for less remuneration.

The Lieven wine-coolers

14. A Pair of Fine Regency Wine-Coolers

Silver gilt
London, 1813
Maker's mark of **Paul Storr**, retailed by **Rundell, Bridge & Rundell**, the Royal Goldsmiths
Height: 12 in (30.5 cm)
Weight: 208 oz (6,469 g)

HERALDRY
The cast and applied arms are those of Prince Lieven.

PROVENANCE
Prince Christopher Andreevich Lieven (1774–1838) and his wife Princess Daria von Benckendorff Lieven (1785–1857)

Prince Christopher Andreevich Lieven was born into a family of Baltic nobility. He entered the Russian army at fifteen in an artillery regiment, and rose through the ranks with lightning speed, eventually becoming aide-de-camp to Emperor Paul I of Russia, and finally director of the Emperor's Mobile Field Chancellery. In 1800, he married Daria (Dorothea) von Benckendorff, a maid of honour to Empress Maria Fyodorovna. The pair moved to London, where Prince Lieven served as the Russian ambassador to the Court of St James. During their years in London, Prince and Princess Lieven established themselves among the capital's glittering social and political elite.

Dorothea, Princess Lieven, stipple engraving by Frederick Christian Lewis Sr, after Sir Thomas Lawrence
© National Portrait Gallery, London

Dorothea Lieven, a Baltic Russian raised in the court of Catherine the Great, was a woman about whom it was impossible to be neutral. "There never figured on the Courtly stage a female intriguer more restless, more arrogant, more mischievous, more (politically, and therefore we mean it not offensively) odious than this supercilious Ambassadress," said a rival. "It is not fashionable," she informed her lover, the Austrian Chancellor, Prince Metternich, "where I am not." She was also reputed to have had an affair with Lord Palmerston, although there is no firm proof.

"This beautiful England," she wrote to her brother on arriving for the first time, "is always the same – an endless chain of perfections which appeal to the reason but leave the imagination untouched." England is not, she concluded, "the country of emotions."

A rum barrel for a royal admiral

15. A George IV Barrel-Form Urn

Silver
London, 1823
Maker's mark of **John Bridge** of the Royal Goldsmiths **Rundell, Bridge & Rundell**
Height: 15 ⅛ in (38.4 cm)
Gross weight: 121 oz 10 dwt (3,780 g)

PROVENANCE
William, Duke of Clarence, later William IV (1765–1837)
Property from a Kentucky Estate, Christie's, New York, October 27, 1992, lot 230

William, Duke of Clarence, later King William IV, after John Hoppner. © *National Portrait Gallery, London*

The rum-barrel form of this urn was especially appropriate for the third son of King George and Queen Charlotte, who made a career in the Royal Navy. In 1823, the year this barrel was commissioned, he began his second term as Admiral of the Fleet. He was appointed Lord High Admiral in 1828.

With the death in 1818 of Princess Charlotte, only child of the Prince Regent, a royal marriage race had begun between the younger sons of George III, collectively known as the Royal Dukes, in order to produce an heir to the throne. William, Duke of Clarence, had been in a long-standing relationship with a mistress, as he, like his brothers, had not been able to afford a wife. In his case, Dorothy Jordan, an actress, had produced a large brood of children with the duke and by continuing her successful acting career between pregnancies had managed to support both the duke and their family. But with his duty to produce an heir to the throne before him, the duke severed all ties with Mrs Jordan. His lawyers wrote to her requesting the return of the jewellery the duke had given her during their time together. By way of reply, she sent back one of her playbills, with the words at the bottom *NO REFUNDS MADE AFTER THE RAISING OF THE CURTAIN* underlined in red.

The duke found a wife in one of the daughters of the King of Saxe-Meiningen who proved to be a loyal consort to him after he succeeded to the throne as King William IV in 1830. The marriage produced no children, however, and it was to be the eighteen-year-old daughter of his younger brother, the Duke of Kent, who would succeed him as Queen Victoria in 1837.

In stark contrast to his brother George IV, William was a bluff sailor to the end of his life, dismissing his brother's art collection as "knickknackery". Without doubt the admiral enjoyed the fact that this tea urn is in the form of a naval "rum tub". Since 1655 British sailors had enjoyed their daily rum ration of half a pint. The tradition continued until 1970.

Rarity and elegance

16. Charles II Royal Presentation Ewer

Silver gilt
London, c. 1667
Maker's mark 'HW', an escallop below, probably for
Henry Welch
Height: 9 in (23 cm)
Weight: 29 oz 5 dwt (914 g)

HERALDRY
The arms are those of Mercer impaling those of Stewart, for Sir James Mercer of Aldie, a burgess of Perth, who married in 1648, Jean, eldest daughter of Sir Thomas Stewart of Grantully.

Sir James Mercer, whose London house was in Axe Yard, Westminster (where Samuel Pepys lived between August 1658 and July 1660), was appointed Gentleman Usher to Charles II in January 1661. His only son Charles was christened in June 1667 in the presence of his godfather, the king, whose gift of 80 ounces of gilt plate to mark the event is recorded in the Jewel Office warrant books in the National Archives. Writing afterwards to his father-in-law, Mercer recalled that "His Majesty on the occasion was very jovial, without any sort of drinking". This elegant ewer was part of that royal gift.

The Mercers' Scottish seat, Aldie Castle (pronounced locally as Audie), stands on the northern slopes of a glen in the parish of Fossaway, Kinross-shire. It is a fortified house, in the style typical of sixteenth-century Scottish baronial strongholds. A local legend recounts how Sir James Mercer condemned one of his grooms to be executed for stealing a bowl of corn. The man was hanged on an old tree and with his dying breath uttered the curse that the Mercers would have no male heirs for nineteen generations. Sure enough, Aldie passed through the female line nineteen times until, some three centuries later, Emily Jane Mercer married Henry, the fourth Marquess of Lansdowne, who took the name Mercer Nairne. They had a son, the fifth marquess, and the curse was finally broken.

The maker's mark on this ewer has been attributed by the silver historian Christopher Hartop to Henry Welch, an immigrant craftsman who evidently worked for the royal household. The mark appears on a pair of candlesticks in Lambeth Palace Chapel, and on another in the Fogg Art Museum, Harvard University.

The Gladstone Dinner Service

17. A Magnificent George IV Presentation Dinner Service

Silver
London, 1824
Maker's mark of Paul Storr

Comprising:
A pair of six-light candelabra
A pair of soup tureens and covers
Four oblong entrée dishes and covers on Sheffield Plate stands
Four oval entreé dishes and covers on Sheffield Plate stands
Four wine-coolers modelled on the Warwick Vase
Two sets of four salts and spoons
Four sauce tureens and covers
A pair of second-course dishes
A graduated set of ten meat dishes
A pair of salvers
A seven-piece tea and coffee service

Total weight 3,349 oz 3 dwt (104,078 g)

HERALDRY
The arms are those of Gladstone impaling Robertson, for Sir John Gladstone (1764–1851) and his second wife Anne MacKenzie, the daughter of Andrew Robertson, whom he married in 1800.

PROVENANCE
Presented to Sir John Gladstone (1764–1851) on Monday, October 18, 1824, following a public subscription raised by the people of Liverpool
Then by descent in the family until 2013

PUBLISHED
"Varieties", *Liverpool Mercury*, October 22, 1824

Complete dinner services from any period in English silver are extremely rare, and with the exception of the one made for the Earl of Egremont of Petworth and another made for the Duke of Norfolk, this is the only service by Storr to survive more or less complete.

The son of an Edinburgh merchant, Sir John Gladstone began as a clerk in a Liverpool trading house. In time he became a partner and made a fortune as the Liverpool trade burgeoned during the Napoleonic Wars. He was a generous benefactor of the city of Liverpool and the Gladstone Docks are named after him. In old age he retired to Fasque, his estate in Scotland. His third son was the politician William Ewart Gladstone, who served as Prime Minister four times during Queen Victoria's reign.

Sir John Gladstone (1764–1851) by William Bradley, Walker Art Gallery.
Image by Public Catalogue Foundation, courtesy National Museums Liverpool

Koopman Rare Art | 45

The Gladstone Service
Four vegetable dishes and covers on Sheffield
Plate stands

The Gladstone Service
Salts from the set of eight

The Gladstone Service
Four entrée dishes and covers on
Sheffield Plate stands

The Gladstone Service
Four Warwick Vase wine-coolers

The Gladstone Service
Four sauce tureens and covers

The Gladstone Service
Pair of soup tureens and covers

The Gladstone Service
Seven-piece tea and coffee service

Detail of one of the pair of wine-coolers by Paul Storr, no. 6